Spotlight on Brazil

Bobbie Kalman

🍄 Crabtree Publishing Company

www.crabtreebooks.com

Spotlight On My Country

Created by Bobbie Kalman

For my longtime friend Tony Zinnanti and
his Brazilian family, Alba and Bianca,
with much love to you all

**Author and
Editor-in-Chief**
Bobbie Kalman

Editors
Kathy Middleton
Crystal Sikkens

Fact editor
Marcella Haanstra

Photo research
Bobbie Kalman

Design
Bobbie Kalman
Katherine Berti
Samantha Crabtree (cover)

**Print and production coordinator
and prepress technician**
Katherine Berti

Photographs
Corel: pages 19 (bottom left), 23 (bottom
    left)
Dreamstime: pages 22 (bottom left), 24,
    25 (top right and bottom right)
Wikipedia: Francisco Aurélio de Figueiredo
    e Melo: page 12 (bottom left); Martin
    St-Amant-CC-BY-SA-3.0: pages 14–15;
    Malene Thyssen, http://commons.
    wikimedia.org/wiki/user:Malene:
    page 21 (top left); Pontanegra:
    page 29 (top left)
Other images by Shutterstock

Library and Archives Canada Cataloguing in Publication

Kalman, Bobbie, 1947-
    Spotlight on Brazil / Bobbie Kalman.

(Spotlight on my country)
Includes index.
Issued also in electronic format.
ISBN 978-0-7787-3461-1 (bound).--ISBN 978-0-7787-3487-1 (pbk.)

    1. Brazil--Juvenile literature. I. Title. II. Series: Spotlight on
my country

F2508.5.K34 2011   j981   C2011-900068-7

Library of Congress Cataloging-in-Publication Data

Kalman, Bobbie.
    Spotlight on Brazil / Bobbie Kalman.
        p. cm. -- (Spotlight on my country)
    Includes index.
    ISBN 978-0-7787-3487-1 (pbk. : alk. paper) -- ISBN 978-0-7787-3461-1
(reinforced library binding : alk. paper) -- ISBN 978-1-4271-9684-2
(electronic (pdf))
    1. Brazil--Juvenile literature. I. Title. II. Series.

    F2508.5.K35 2011
    981--dc22
                                                    2010051955

Crabtree Publishing Company
www.crabtreebooks.com   1-800-387-7650

Printed in the U.S.A./022011/CJ20101228

Published in Canada
Crabtree Publishing
616 Welland Ave.
St. Catharines, Ontario
L2M 5V6

Published in the United States
Crabtree Publishing
PMB 59051
350 Fifth Avenue, 59th Floor
New York, New York 10118

Published in the United Kingdom
Crabtree Publishing
Maritime House
Basin Road North, Hove
BN41 1WR

Published in Australia
Crabtree Publishing
386 Mt. Alexander Rd.
Ascot Vale (Melbourne)
VIC 3032

Contents

Welcome to Brazil!   4

The coast of Brazil   6

Old and new capitals   8

Important cities   10

Brazil's history   12

The land of Brazil   14

The Amazon River   16

Amazon plants   18

Rainforest animals   20

The people of Brazil   22

Indigenous peoples   24

Religion in Brazil   26

Brazil's culture   28

Brazil's big parties!   30

Glossary and Index   32

Welcome to Brazil!

Brazil is a **country** in South America. A country is an area of land with borders. Brazil shares its borders with Venezuela, Guyana, Suriname, French Guiana, Colombia, Bolivia, Peru, Argentina, Paraguay, and Uruguay. It is the biggest country in South America and the only Portuguese-speaking country on the **continent** of South America. A continent is a huge area of land. The other continents on Earth are Europe, Asia, Africa, North America, Antarctica, and Australia/Oceania. Brazil's capital city is Brasília.

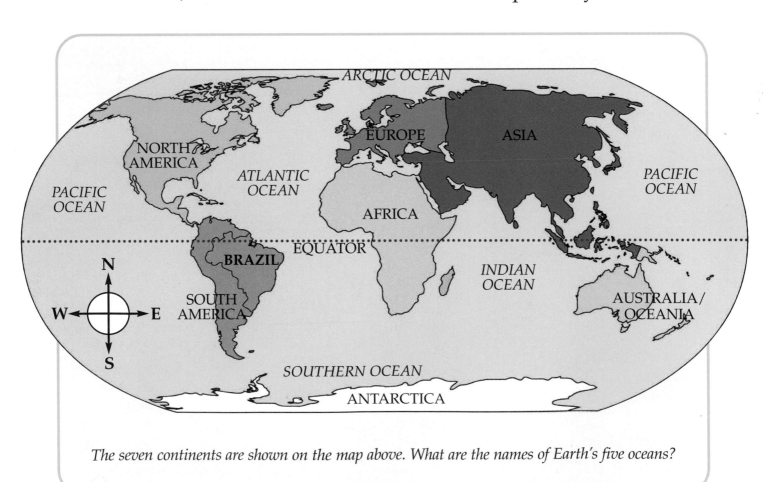

The seven continents are shown on the map above. What are the names of Earth's five oceans?

VENEZUELA

GUYANA

SURINAME

FRENCH GUIANA

ATLANTIC OCEAN

COLOMBIA

Amazon rain forest

EQUATOR

ECUADOR

Amazonas

Parintins

Belém

Manaus

Amazon River

Amazon rain forest

Amazon rain forest

Natal

Recife

BRAZIL

PERU

Diamond Highlands

Salvador

Pantanal

Brasília

Bahia

BOLIVIA

Mato Grosso
do Sul

GUANABARA BAY

PARAGUAY

São Paulo

Rio de Janeiro

Iguaçú Falls

PACIFIC OCEAN

ARGENTINA

URUGUAY

CHILE

N

W E

S

*Most of Brazil is south of the **equator**, an imaginary line around the middle of Earth. The seasons south of the equator are opposite to those in North America. Brazil's summer is from December to March. It is the rainiest time of the year. Brazil's winter is much drier. It is from June to September.*

The coast of Brazil

Brazil has a very long **coastline** along the Atlantic Ocean. A **coast** is where land meets an ocean. A coastline is the line between continents and oceans. It is the outline of a coast. Long white beaches lie along the coast of Brazil. **Islands** of all sizes dot the ocean waters. Many Brazilian cities, such as Rio de Janeiro shown here, are built on **bays** that are sheltered from powerful ocean winds and water **currents**. A current is a body of water that moves in a certain direction.

A bay is an area where a coast curves inward. The water in a bay is calmer than water in the open ocean.

Thousands of people come to swim on Copacabana Beach. It has beautiful white sand.

Sugar Loaf Mountain is at the entrance to Guanabara Bay. The bay has sandy beaches.

Old and new capitals

Salvador, Brazil's first capital city has colorful old buildings and many **mansions**, or large homes. Like most of Brazil's large cities, it is on the Atlantic coast. Brazil's second capital was Rio de Janeiro. It is also on the coast. The present capital city, Brasília, is located about 560 miles (900 km) from the Atlantic.

Brasília

Salvador

Rio de Janeiro

The city of Salvador has a Lower City and an Upper City. The Lower City is at ocean level, but the Upper City sits high above the ocean. This picture shows the Upper City.

Modern Brasília

The present capital city of Brasília was chosen by the government to encourage people to move inland. The city was planned in the shape of an airplane. The body of the plane is made up of government buildings, and the wings are made up of large city squares. Each city square has tall apartment buildings, shops, schools, and open fields.

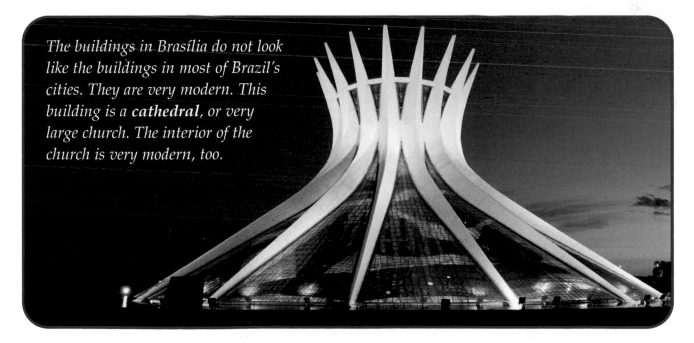

The buildings in Brasília do not look like the buildings in most of Brazil's cities. They are very modern. This building is a **cathedral**, *or very large church. The interior of the church is very modern, too.*

Important cities

Rio de Janeiro is Brazil's most famous city. It was the capital of the country until 1960. It is still the capital city of the State of Rio de Janeiro and the second-largest city in Brazil. Italian explorer Amerigo Vespucci gave Rio its name. Vespucci was the first European to land at Guanabara Bay. He named the area Rio de Janeiro, which means "River of January." Vespucci thought the bay was a river, and he arrived on the first day of January. The city of Rio de Janeiro sits on the mountains that surround the bay. The most famous mountain is Sugar Loaf. In the past, the mountains were covered with rain forests.

The cone-shaped mountain called Sugar Loaf looks like the clay molds that were once used to purify sugar.

Busy São Paulo

São Paulo is Brazil's largest city. This huge city (and surrounding areas) has a **population** of close to 20 million people. São Paulo was the second permanent Portuguese colony in the **New World**, or North and South America. It is the most multicultural city in Brazil. People of German, Portuguese, Japanese, Italian, Spanish, and African **descent** live there.

São Paulo has many very tall buildings.

*Recife is Brazil's fourth-largest city. Old churches and markets from long ago combine with modern **skyscrapers**. Recife is also known for its beautiful **coral reefs** in the ocean close to shore.*

Brazil's history

The first Brazilians were **indigenous**, or native, peoples. It was believed that they came from Asia to North America and then moved south to what is now Brazil. In the 1400s, **explorers** from Portugal and Spain were sailing on the Atlantic Ocean looking for new lands. Portuguese sea captain Pedro Álvares Cabral claimed Brazil as a **colony** of Portugal. The Portuguese looked for **natural resources** and found brazilwood trees, which were used to make red dye. In the 1500s, many indigenous people were captured and forced to work as **slaves** on sugar cane **plantations**. Traders then started bringing slaves from Africa to work in mines, after gold and diamonds were discovered. The money made from mining was used to start coffee plantations. Coffee was Brazil's next important product.

Pedro Álvares Cabral claimed Brazil for Portugal.

sugar cane

sugar

diamonds

coffee beans

12

The Republic of Brazil

Brazil gained its independence from Portugal in 1822, when Dom Pedro, son of Portugal's king, became Brazil's emperor. In 1889, the emperor fled, and the country went through some hard times. Today, Brazil is among the top economic countries in the world. Its government is a **democratic republic**. In a democratic republic, people vote for the person they want as their **president**, or leader. Brazil's new president is a woman named Dilma Rousseff. She started her four-year term in office in January 2011.

The national flag of Brazil is a blue disc showing a starry sky. A curved band across it contains Brazil's national motto, "Ordem e Progresso," which means "Order and Progress." This flag became Brazil's national flag in 1889.

(below) The government buildings in Brasília look very modern, like the rest of the city. The National Congress building is made up of two towers and two domes. The members of the National Congress make Brazil's laws.

The land of Brazil

Brazil's land has everything—**rain forests**, **wetlands**, **deserts**, **grasslands**, and **mountains**. The Pantanal is a tropical wetland. It is the world's largest wetland. It lies mostly within the Brazilian state of Mato Grosso do Sul. A wetland is land that is covered with water for part or all of the year. Brazil also has dry deserts that have long periods without rain. Brazil has many forests, too. The Amazon rain forest is just one kind of forest in Brazil. There are also forests close to the Atlantic coast, where many kinds of birds and monkeys live. Tall mountains can be found in Brazil's **highlands**. Brazil also has many rivers with huge waterfalls, such as Iguaçú Falls, shown below.

Iguaçú Falls is made up of 275 waterfalls and sits on the border of Brazil and Argentina, along the Iguaçú River.

The Diamond Highlands contain some very steep **cliffs**. Cliffs are rocky edges of mountains overlooking **valleys**, or low areas.

This cow is brave to walk among crocodiles called caimans, which live in the Pantanal!

The Amazon River

The Amazon River starts in Peru and ends at the Atlantic Ocean. On its way to the Atlantic Ocean, it is joined by more than 1,000 **tributaries**. A tributary is a small river that flows into a larger one. The Amazon is not the world's longest river, but it is the largest because it carries the most water. About one-fifth of Earth's water is carried by the Amazon. The Amazon River empties into the Atlantic Ocean north of the city of Belém.

Parts of the Amazon River flood during the rainy season. People who live in these areas build homes on **stilts**. Stilts are poles that keep a house above water.

The Amazon River dolphin lives in the freshwater of the Amazon River. This pink dolphin has been listed as **endangered**. Endangered means it is in danger of disappearing from Earth.

Amazon plants

Thousands of **species**, or types, of plants grow in the Amazon rain forest. The rain forest has more than 2,500 species of **flowering plants**, or plants with flowers, fruits, and seeds. Many more species have not yet been discovered. People feel that some of the plants in the Amazon could be used in medicines to cure many diseases. Unfortunately, much of the rain forest has been cut down to make room for cattle ranches. Cutting down the rain forest also results in there being less oxygen on Earth. Oxygen is a gas in the air that people and animals need to breathe.

Hot lips flowers and leaves have a pleasant smell and attract bees, hummingbirds, and butterflies. A spider is sitting on the bottom "lip" of this flower.

Victoria water lilies grow in ponds fed by the Amazon River. They are so big that a small child could float on top of one of them.

Huge vines climb woody rainforest plants. Some vines store fresh, cool water that is pure enough to drink.

The Amazon rain forest is very important to Earth. One-fifth of the oxygen on Earth is produced by the trees of this rain forest.

Rainforest animals

Toucans are known for their large bills, which are almost as large as their bodies.

Thousands of species of animals live in Brazil's rain forest. There are more than 1,600 species of birds, 230 kinds of snakes, 600 kinds of mammals, 40 kinds of turtles, and 70,000 kinds of insects. Scientists believe that millions more have yet to be discovered. Some animals live high up in the trees, and some live on the ground.

A blue morpho butterfly is larger than a person's hand!

Parrots are colorful birds. There are more than 370 kinds!

The golden lion tamarin is a type of monkey—not a lion. This mother and baby live high in the trees.

This two-toed sloth and its baby are hanging upside down from a tree branch.

This margay cat lives high up in rainforest trees.
It is a skillful climber.

This tarantula has trapped a tree frog to eat.
Turantulas are big hairy spiders.

The coati is part of the
raccoon family, but it has
a piglike nose.

The Amazon leaf frog
lives in trees. It is a
good climber.

Tapirs can be found
near water in the
Amazon rain forest.

Capybaras are the world's
biggest **rodents**. They are
good swimmers.

Anaconda snakes
can eat animals as
big as jaguars!

The jaguar is the largest **predator**
in the Amazon rain forest.

The people of Brazil

Brazilians come from different ethnic groups and have different customs and cultures. Almost half the people in South America live in Brazil. The population is more than 190 million people. Portuguese is Brazil's official language, but other languages are also spoken. Brazil has one of the world's fastest-growing economies, but many people in Brazil still do not have proper homes in which to live.

*This young soccer player's heritage is European. Her **ancestors** are German.*

Many indigenous people live in Brazil. These girls live in the Amazon rain forest. They are Ka'apor Indians.

(above) This happy baby just had her first birthday. Her mother hopes her child will have a bright future.

(left) This student is using a computer at a university library. She is studying to become a teacher.

Many people's ancestors came from Africa. About 80 percent of the people who live in the city of Salvador are of African heritage.

Brazil is home to the largest Japanese population outside of Japan. More than one million Japanese people live in Brazil, including this soccer player.

Indigenous peoples

Several hundred thousand indigenous peoples, belonging to 234 groups, live in Brazil. Many live in villages in the Amazon rain forest. Some live traditional lives, following the ways their people lived for thousands of years. Others combine old and new ways. The largest group is the Guarani. Forty to fifty thousand Guarani live in both Brazil and Paraguay. The Kamayurá and Ka'apor tribes live in the Amazonian Basin of Brazil. Indigenous people are fighting hard to keep their traditional ways of life, but their villages are being surrounded by big changes, such as logging, mining, and cattle ranching.

This picture shows a Ka'apor family in their Amazon village. Their name Ka'apor means "footprints in the woods." These people find their food, water, and happiness in the Amazon rain forest.

These native rainforest girls are wearing traditional clothing, including feather headpieces.

This young Ka'apor fisherman caught a fish from his canoe. It will feed his family.

In a Kamayurá village, a **tapuwí**, or "house of the flutes," contains musical instruments that only the men play. The men also discuss fishing trips or plan festivals in a meeting area in front of this music house.

These native Indian children are sitting at the doorway of their rainforest home.

Religion in Brazil

The Portuguese **settlers** who came to Brazil in the 1500s brought their religion, Roman Catholicism, with them. Roman Catholicism is a Christian religion based on the teachings of Jesus Christ. Some religious traditions in Brazil combine Christian beliefs with indigenous or African customs. This huge statue of Jesus, called "Christ the Redeemer," shows Jesus holding his arms out as if to embrace the people of Rio de Janeiro.

This statue of Jesus is 124 feet (38 meters) tall. It stands at the peak of Corcovado Mountain, overlooking Rio de Janeiro.

Yemanjá, the Goddess of the Sea, is honored all along the coast of Bahia, but the largest festival in her honor takes place on the beach in Salvador. Thousands of people come to leave their offerings. Girls dressed in white carry gifts for Yemanjá. Some gifts are taken out to sea. There is singing, dancing, and fireworks. These people are loading the boat with flowers and other gifts.

This girl dressed in white is carrying gifts for Yemanjá.

This building is part of a Buddhist temple. Buddhism was introduced to Brazil by Japanese immigrants. Brazil has the third-largest Buddhist population in the Americas.

Brazil's culture

Culture is the way we live. It is the clothes we wear, the foods we eat, the music we enjoy, the stories we tell, and the ways we celebrate. Brazil is rich in every part of culture—history, art, music, dancing, festivals, and sports. In 2014, Brazil will be hosting the World Cup soccer games, the world's most-watched sporting event. Another event that is watched and copied by the world is Brazil's *Carnaval*, or Carnival, celebrations. Learn more about Brazil's *Carnaval* on pages 30–31.

These drummers are making music at a Carnaval *party.*

This modern building is the Niterói Contemporary Art Museum in Rio de Janeiro.

This building is the Teatro Amazonas, or *Amazon Theater*. This opera house is located in the city of Manaus, inside the Amazon rain forest in Brazil. The Opera Festival is held there every April.

Brazilian musicians such as Carlinhos Brown perform in concerts all over the world. Here, he is singing in Barcelona, Spain.

Capoeira *is part martial arts and part dance. It is a very challenging art. The "dancers" try to make their opponents lose their balance.*

There have been nineteen World Cup soccer tournaments. Brazil has won five times, and Brazil's team is the only one that has played in every tournament. Will Brazil be the big winner in 2014?

Brazil's big parties!

Carnival festivals are held in many countries or cities, but Brazil's *Carnaval* is the biggest in the world. *Carnaval* is celebrated before **Lent**. Lent is a 40-day period of prayer and **fasting**, when many Roman Catholics give up eating certain foods. Brazil's largest *Carnaval* is held in Rio. Weeks before the holiday, musicians and singers lead parades through the streets. There are street parties in which people dance and act silly. The biggest event is the *Carnaval* parade. More than 80,000 spectators watch the parade as Brazil's famous **samba** dance schools compete to see who has the best dancers, musicians, costumes, and floats.

Thousands of people watch the parade from the stands of the stadium that was built for Carnaval.

Bumba Meu Boi

Bumba Meu Boi is a popular festival in Parantins in northern Brazil. It takes place at the end of June and lasts for three days. Like *Carnaval*, there are parades with music and dancers wearing fantastic costumes. Two samba schools compete to put on the best show.

Glossary

Note: Some boldfaced words are defined where they appear in the book.

ancestor A family member from long ago

colony A territory that is controlled by a distant country

coral reef An area of an ocean that is made up of live and dead corals

descendant A person who is related to someone who lived long ago

descent The origin of a person's nationality

desert A dry area with few plants and extremely hot or cold temperatures

endangered Describing a living thing that is in danger of dying out

grassland An area that is covered mainly with grasses and shrubs

highland An area of mountainous land

island Land that has water all around it

natural resource Elements found in nature that are used by humans

plantation A large farm on which one type of crop, such as coffee or sugar, is grown

population The number of people or animals in a certain area

predator An animal that hunts other animals

president The person chosen to lead a government

rodent A mammal with four front teeth that never stop growing

samba A Brazilian dance that came from Africa

settler A person who makes a new home in a place where few other people live

skyscraper A very tall building

slave A person who is forced to work hard for little or no pay

Index

Amazon River 16–17, 19
animals 14, 15, 17, 20–21
bays 6, 7, 10
beaches 6, 7, 27
Brasília 4, 8, 9, 13
Carnaval 28, 30, 31
cities 6, 8–9, 10–11, 13, 16, 23, 29, 30
coasts 6, 8, 14
culture 22, 28–29
dance 29, 30, 31

festivals/celebrations 25, 27, 28, 29, 30–31
flag 13
food 24, 28
government 9, 13
history 12–13, 28
indigenous 12, 22, 24–25
language 22
mountains 7, 10, 14, 15, 26
oceans 4, 6, 11, 12, 16
plants 18–19

population 11, 22, 23, 27
rain forests 10, 14, 18–19, 20–21
religion 26–27
Rio de Janeiro 6, 8, 10, 26, 28, 30
rivers 10, 14, 16–17, 19
Salvador 8, 23, 27
São Paulo 11
soccer 22, 23, 28, 29
villages 24, 25